THE APPLE TREE

ISBN-13: 978-1-4234-2418-5
ISBN-10: 1-4234-2418-2

HAL•LEONARD®
CORPORATION

7777 W. BLUEMOUND RD. P.O. BOX 13819 MILWAUKEE, WI 53213

Visit Hal Leonard Online at
www.halleonard.com

FEELINGS

Words and Music by JERRY BOCK
and SHELDON HARNICK

THE APPLE TREE
(Forbidden Fruit)

Words and Music by JERRY BOCK
and SHELDON HARNICK

Rhythmically

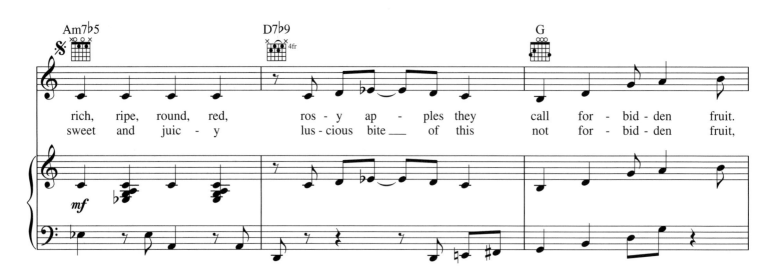

BEAUTIFUL, BEAUTIFUL WORLD

Words and Music by JERRY BOCK
and SHELDON HARNICK

Moderately

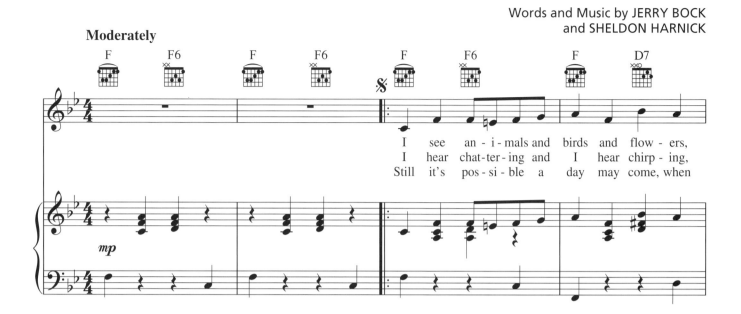

I see an-i-mals and birds and flow-ers,
I hear chat-ter-ing and I hear chirp-ing,
Still it's pos-si-ble a day may come, when

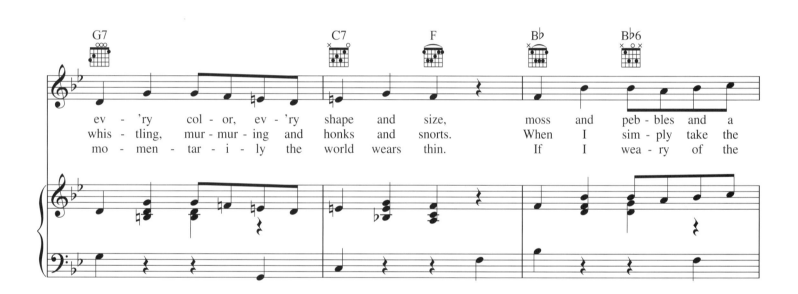

ev-'ry col-or, ev-'ry shape and size, moss and peb-bles and a
whis-tling, mur-mur-ing and honks and snorts. When I sim-ply take the
mo-men-tar-i-ly the world wears thin. If I wea-ry of the

host of won-ders, gleam-ing ev-'ry-where I aim my eyes.
time to lis-ten, I hear mu-sic of a thou-sand sorts.
world out-side me, I can al-ways take a good look in.

WHAT MAKES ME LOVE HIM?

Words and Music by JERRY BOCK
and SHELDON HARNICK

Slowly, in a simple Country Folk style

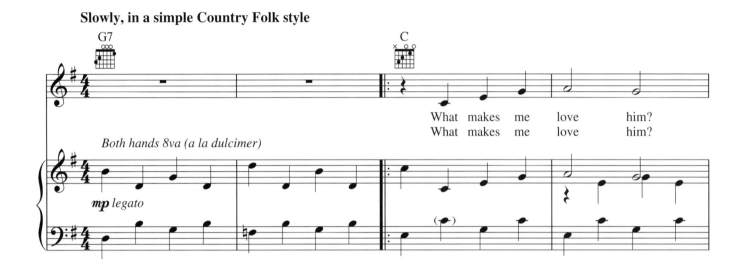

What makes me love him?
What makes me love him?

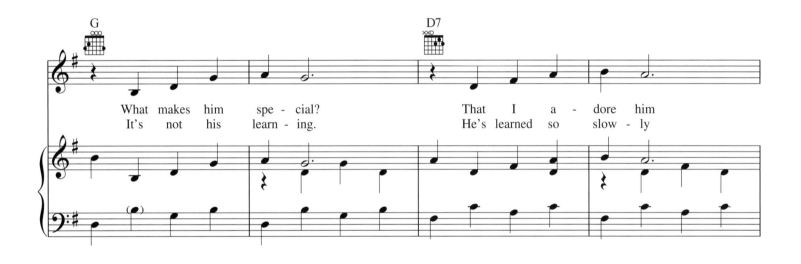

What makes him spe-cial? That I a-dore him
It's not his learn-ing. He's learned so slow-ly

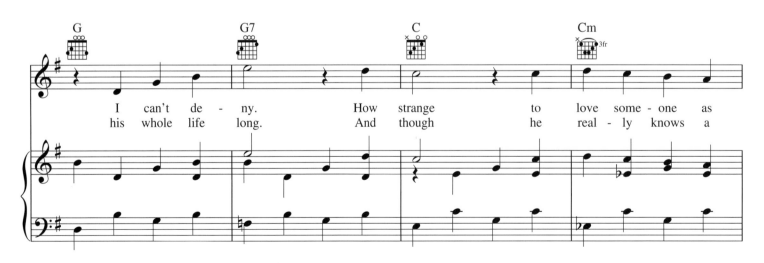

I can't de-ny. How strange to love some-one as
his whole life long. And though he real-ly knows a

I'VE GOT WHAT YOU WANT

Words and Music by JERRY BOCK
and SHELDON HARNICK

Jazz Waltz, Gospel Blues style

I've got what you want. I've got what you need.

I know how much you want it, yeah, yeah. Ba - by,

I know my fa - ther would kill me if he knew my heart was

OH, TO BE A MOVIE STAR

Words and Music by JERRY BOCK
and SHELDON HARNICK

mov - ie star, oh, to be a mov - ie star, a
beau - ti - ful, glam - or - ous, ra - di - ant, rav - ish - ing mov - ie
star. _____
star. _____

GORGEOUS

Words and Music by JERRY BOCK
and SHELDON HARNICK

WEALTH

Words and Music by JERRY BOCK
and SHELDON HARNICK

Move it!

N.C.

f

B7 F#m7   B7b5   B7   Em7

Wealth!
*Wealth   How de-li-cious to

A7b9   Dm7   G7b9

be sur-round-ed   by the com-forts and lux-u-ries ___
out a fire-place,   why de-ny it? It's nice to have, ___

Cmaj7   B7 F#m7   B7b5   B7

that I've nev-er known be-fore. ___ Fame!
but it can-not keep you warm. ___ Fame

*Alternate lyric

YOU ARE NOT REAL

Words and Music by JERRY BOCK
and SHELDON HARNICK

I'M LOST

Words and Music by JERRY BOCK
and SHELDON HARNICK

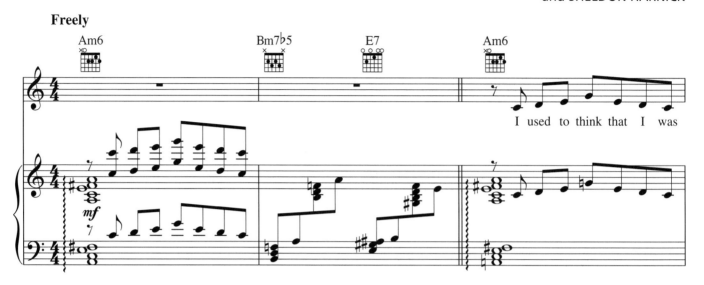

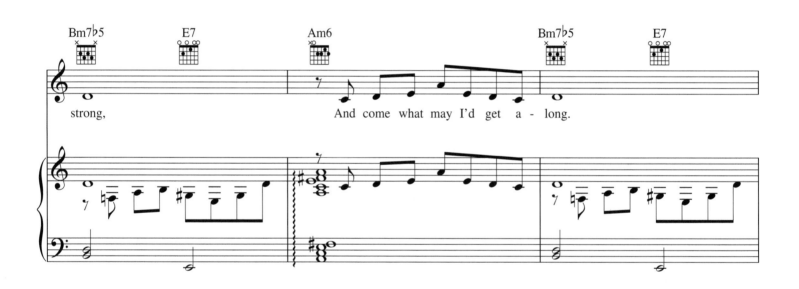

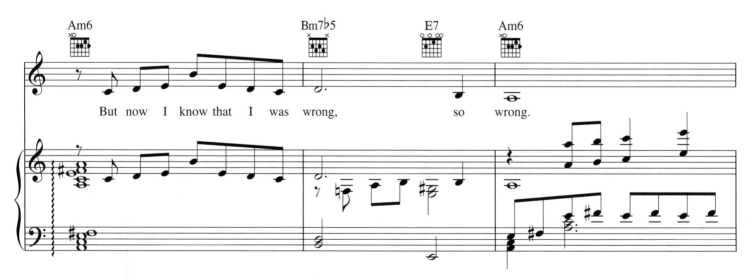

Slow and easy (*a bit plaintive, a bit schmaltzy*)